MINDFUL Colouring BOOK FOR Girls

Inspirational Quotes & Positive Affirmations

Thank you for purchasing this book from amberoctopus, we hope you enjoy it.

Based in rural Buckinghamshire, amberoctopus is a small business created by a father of two young daughters. Our aim is to create engaging books for young people that spark their imagination and creativity – as well as giving parents a little break.

Please consider leaving a review on Amazon. This support will help us create more quality books in the future, thank you very much.

Visit **amberoctopus.com** for more information and to view our full range of books.

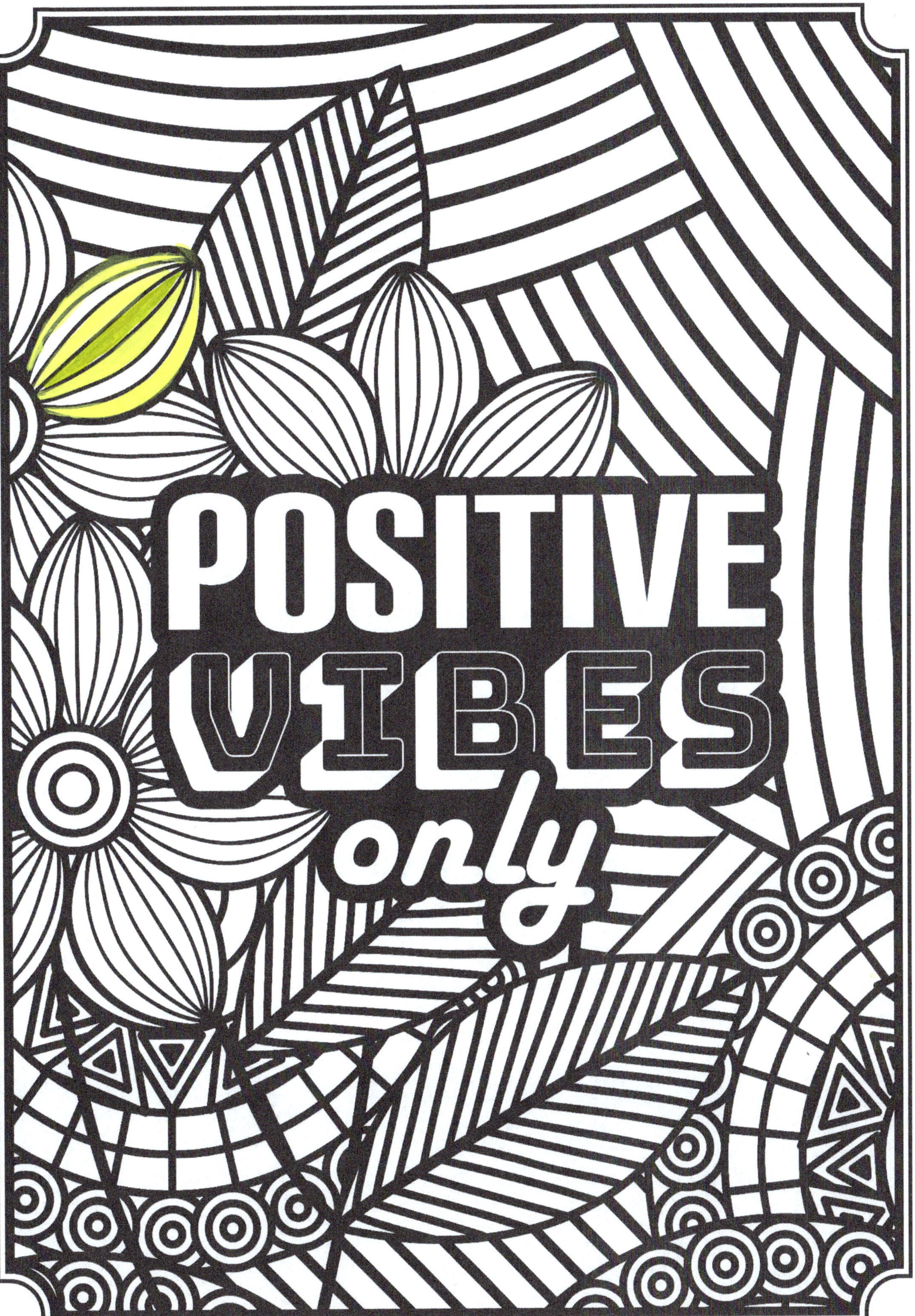
POSITIVE
VIBES
only

Dream
Believe
ACHIEVE

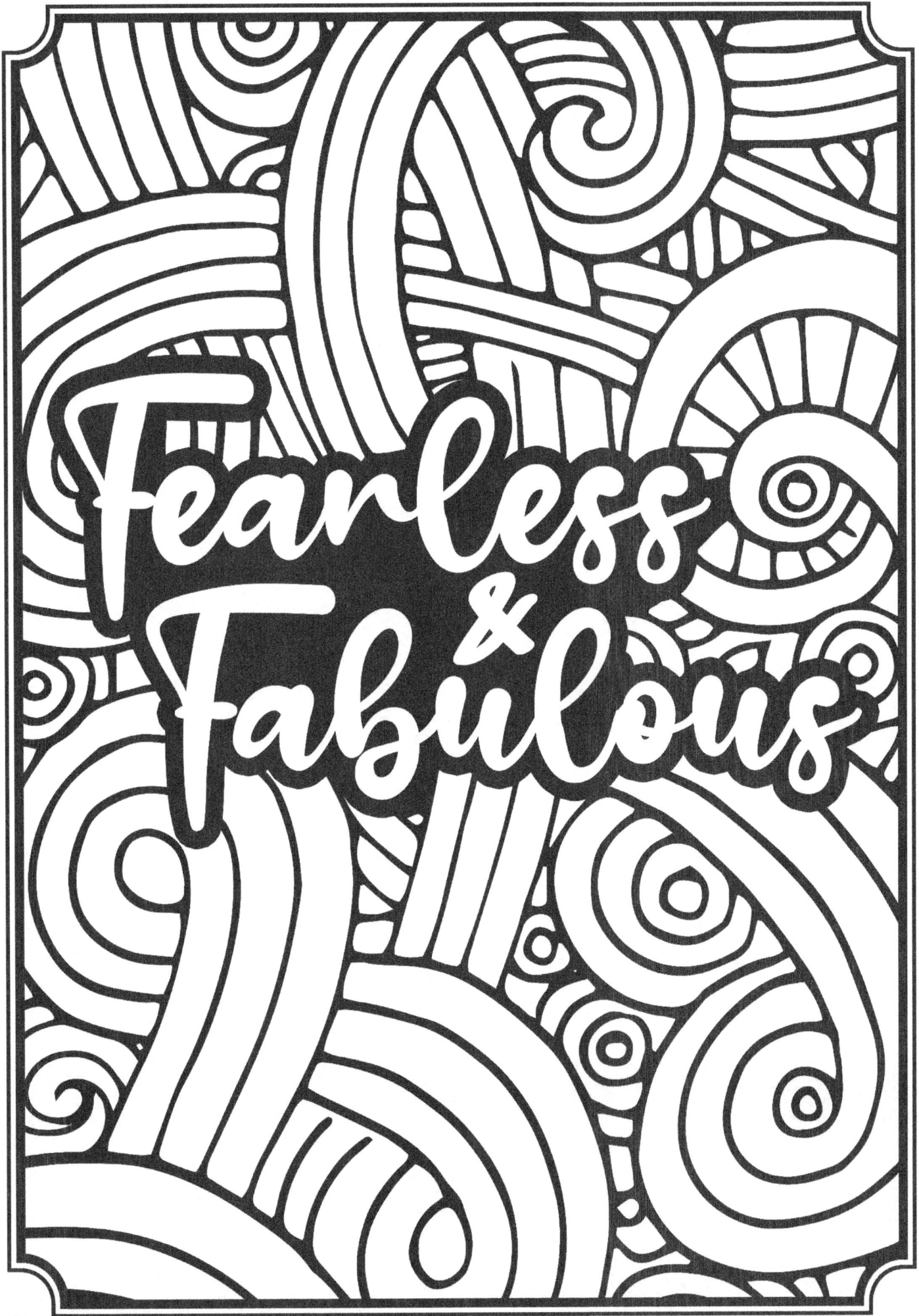

Fearless & Fabulous

BE
BRAVE
be
you

Girls
CAN DO
Anything

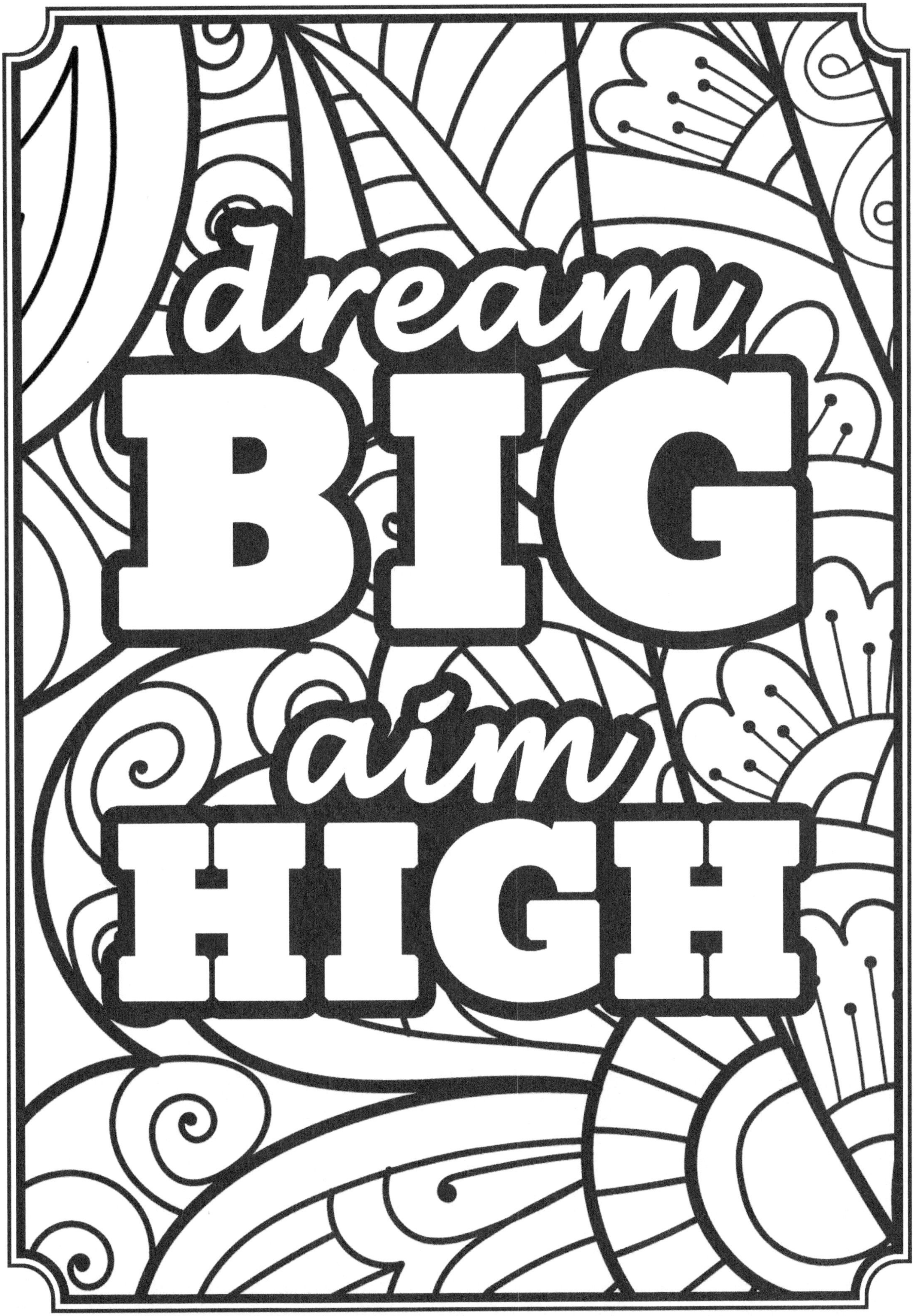
dream
BIG
aim
HIGH

SPARKLE
like you
MEAN IT

KEEP SHINING
Superstar

I am a WARRIOR Princess

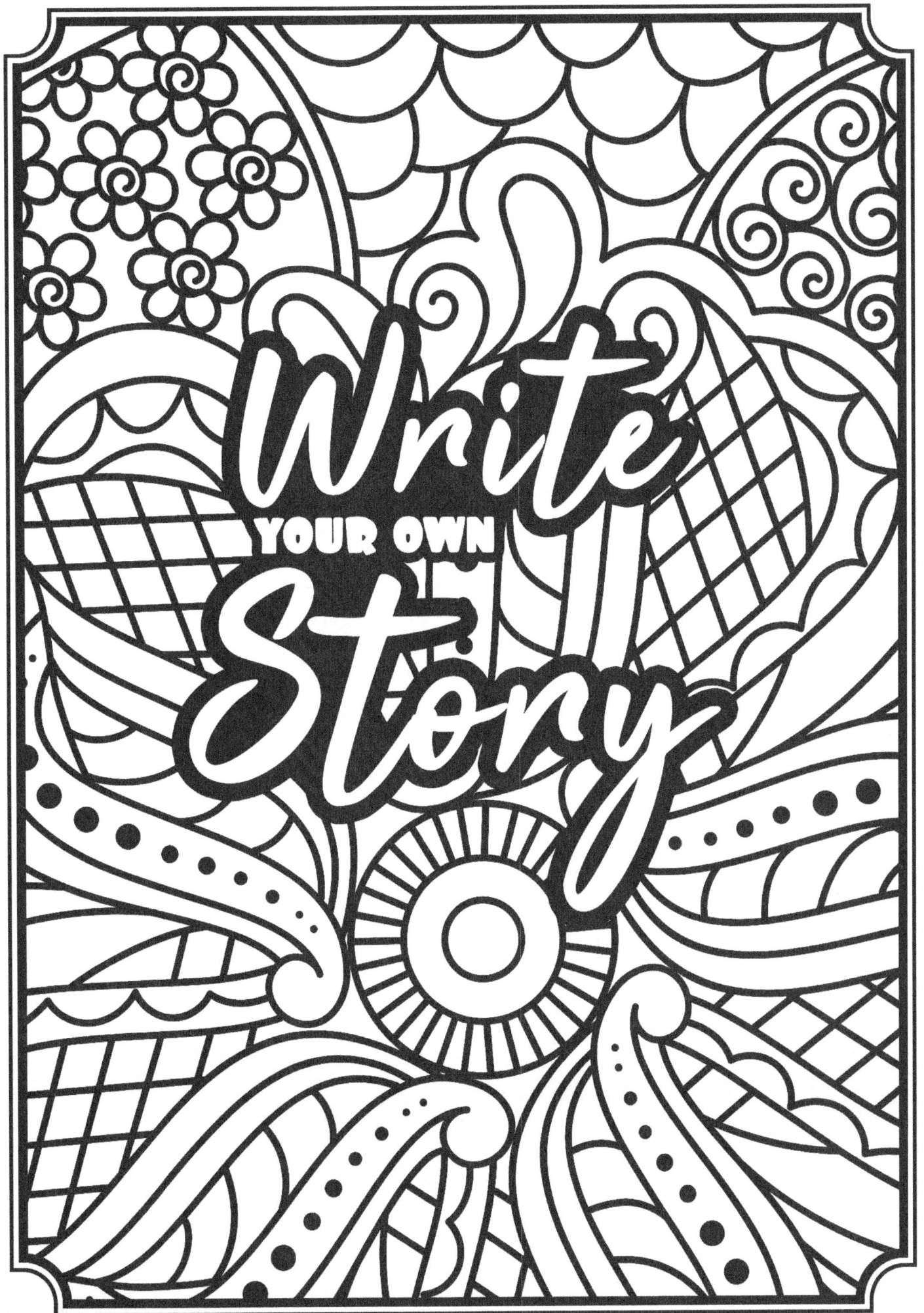

Write YOUR OWN Story

every day
IS A NEW
adventure

I AM SMART CLEVER & CURIOUS

LOVE shines THROUGH ME

BRAVE hearts BIG dreams

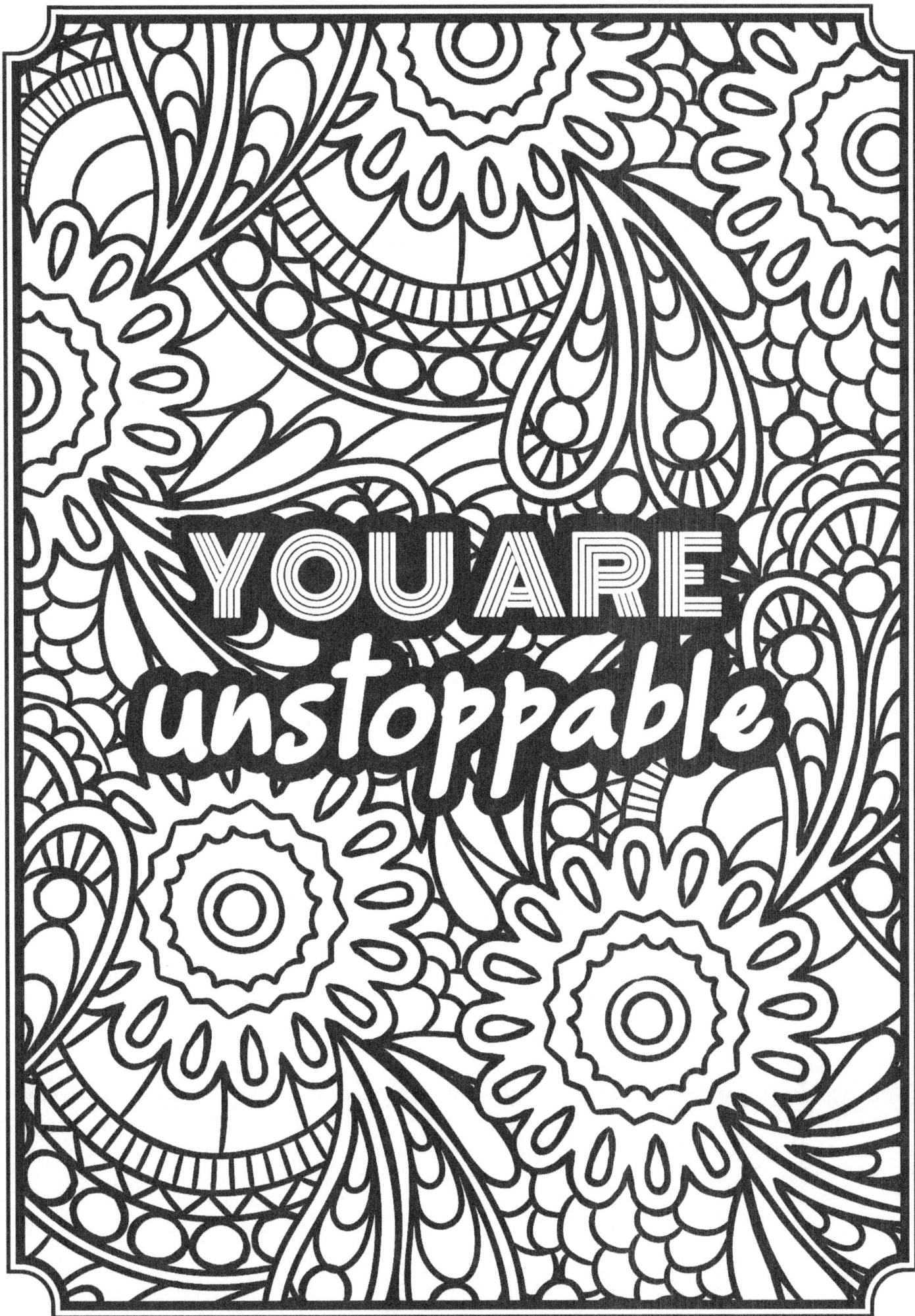

YOU ARE
unstoppable

BUZZING
with kindness and
Love

FIND THE good IN EVERY day

I am
ENOUGH
just as I am

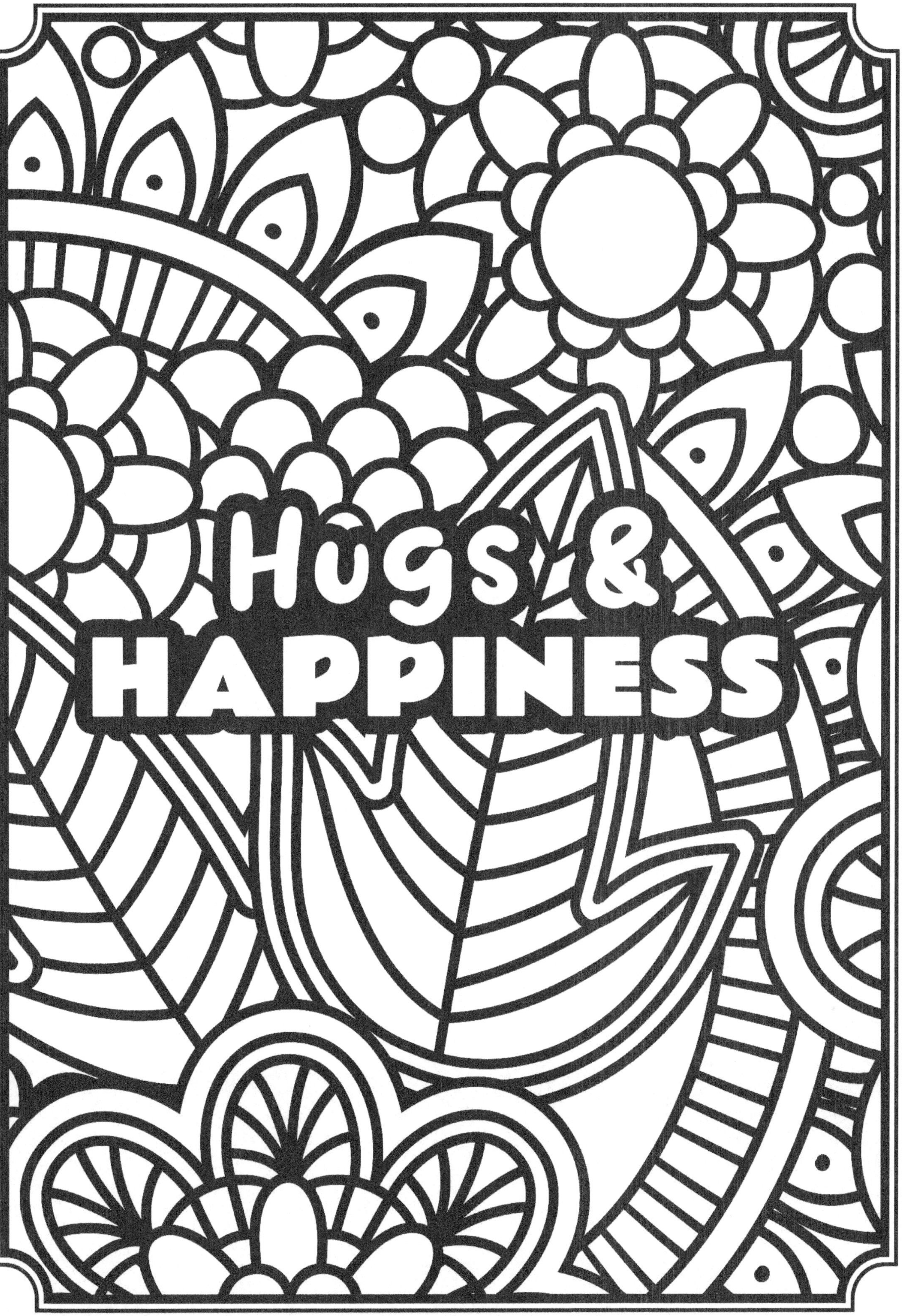
Hugs &
HAPPINESS

I am a
RAINBOW
of
LOVE
and
JOY

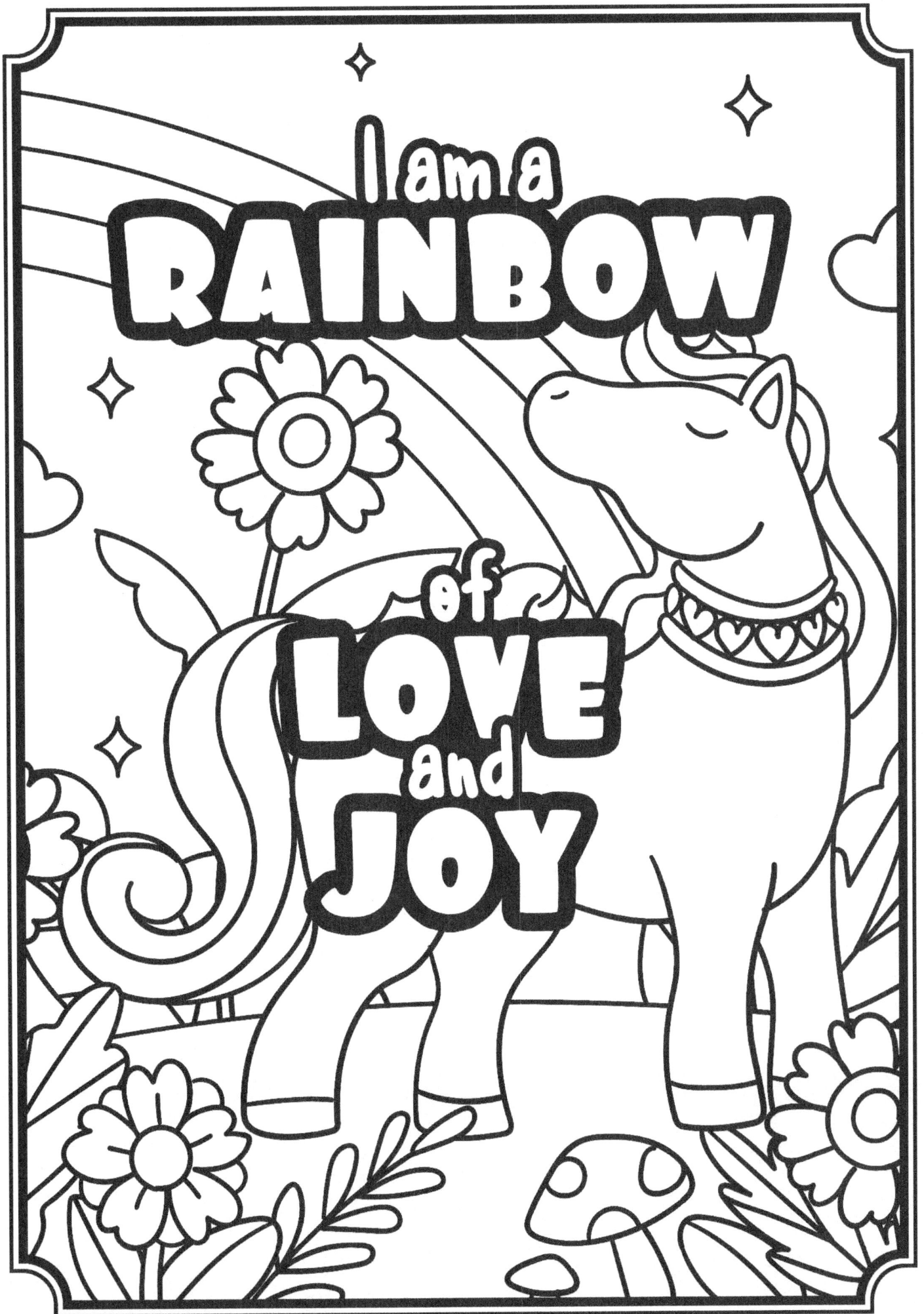

KEEP
GOING
you've
got this

let your LIGHT shine BRIGHT

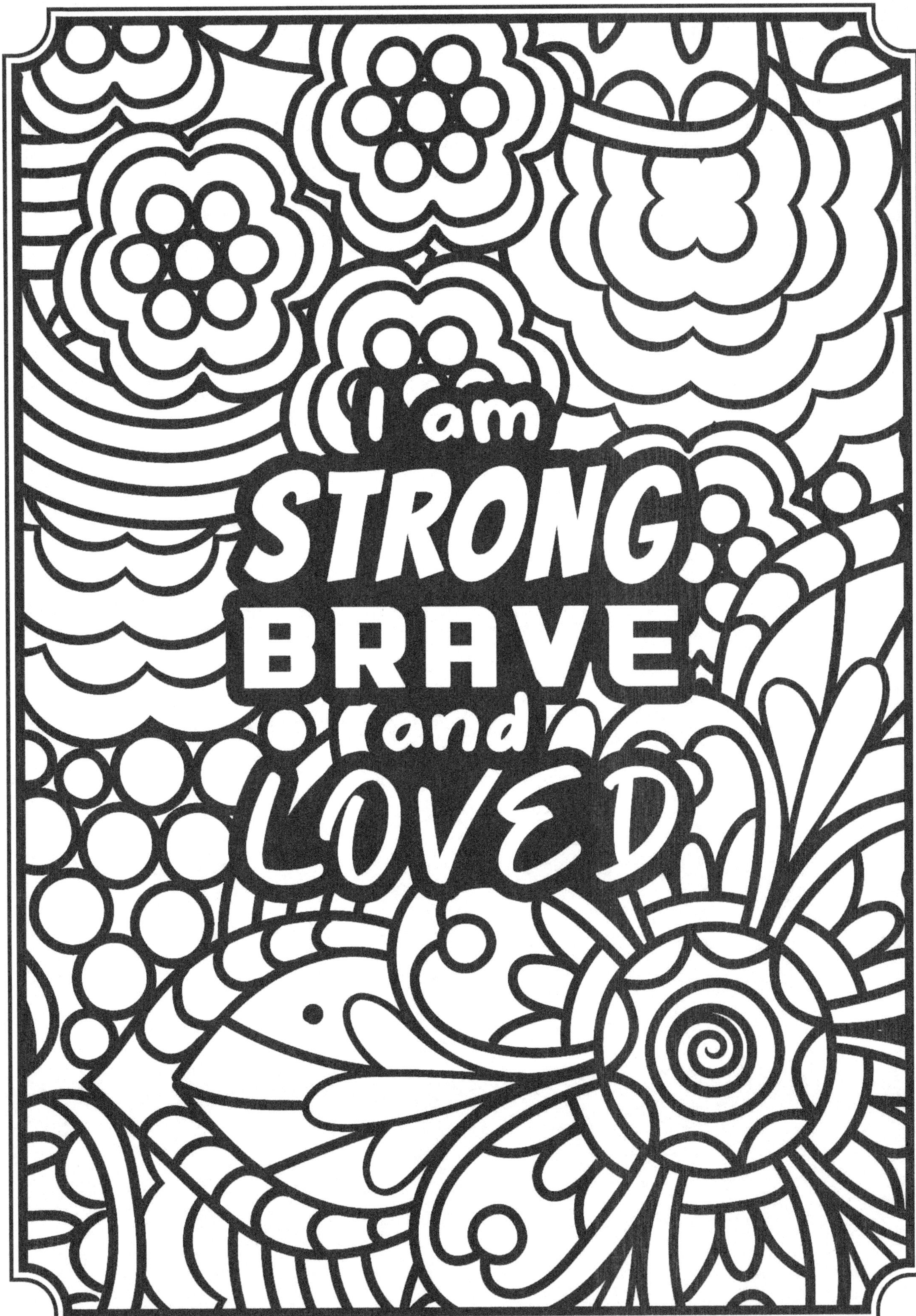
I am
STRONG
BRAVE
and
LOVED

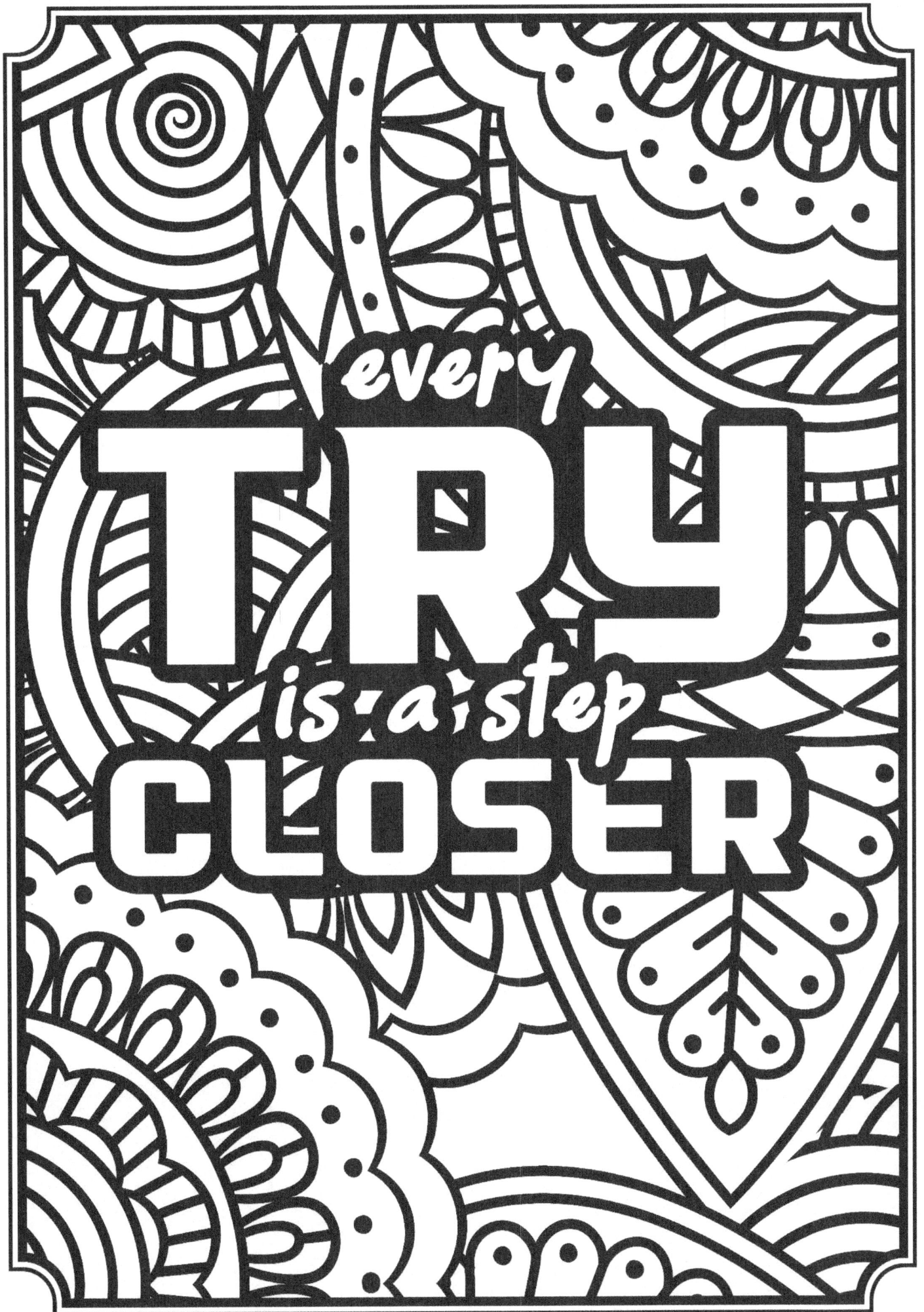

never GIVE UP keep trying

believe in YOURSELF, you're AMAZING

Kindness is my MAGIC potion

I grow STRONGER every day

I create
I imagine
I dream

I am
Beautiful
inside & out

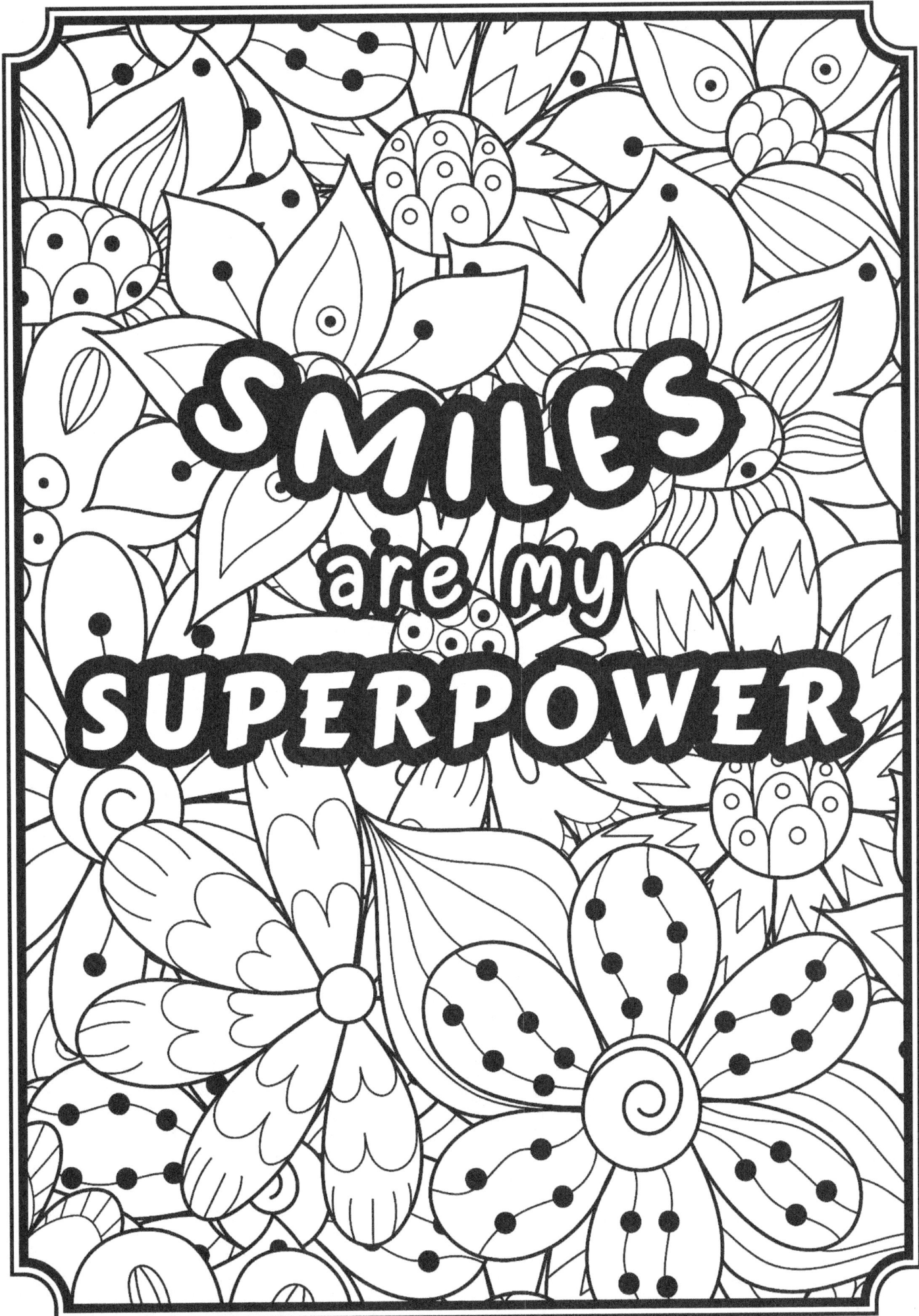

SMILES are my SUPERPOWER

brave girls
SPARKLE
with courage

Fluttering
with grace & beauty

MIRACLES happen every day

I'am a little RAY of SUN shine

sugar SPiCE and all things NICE

I KEEP GOING *even when* things get **Tough**

giggle
MONSTER

I'M PERFECT just the way I AM

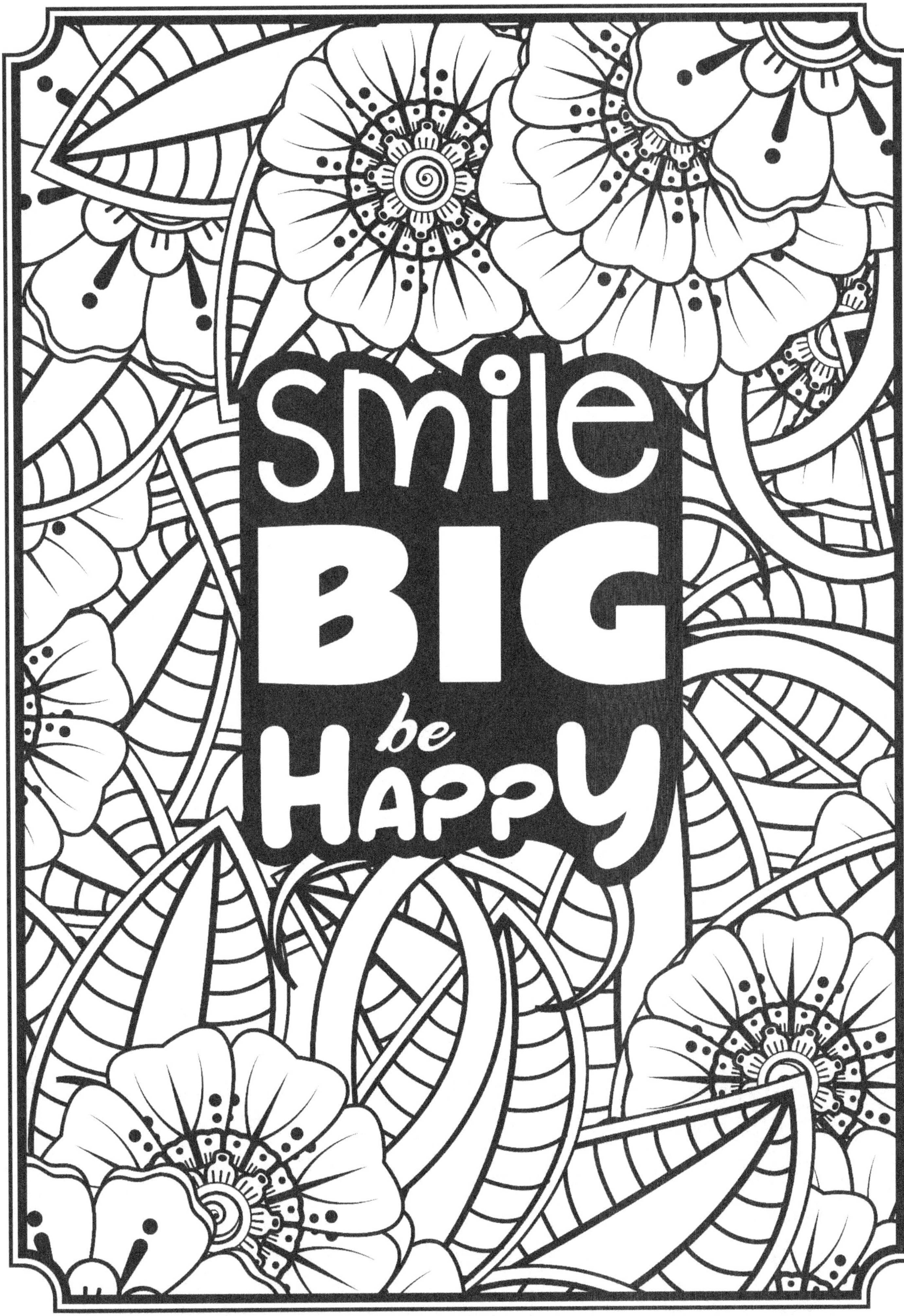
Smile
BIG
be
HAPPY

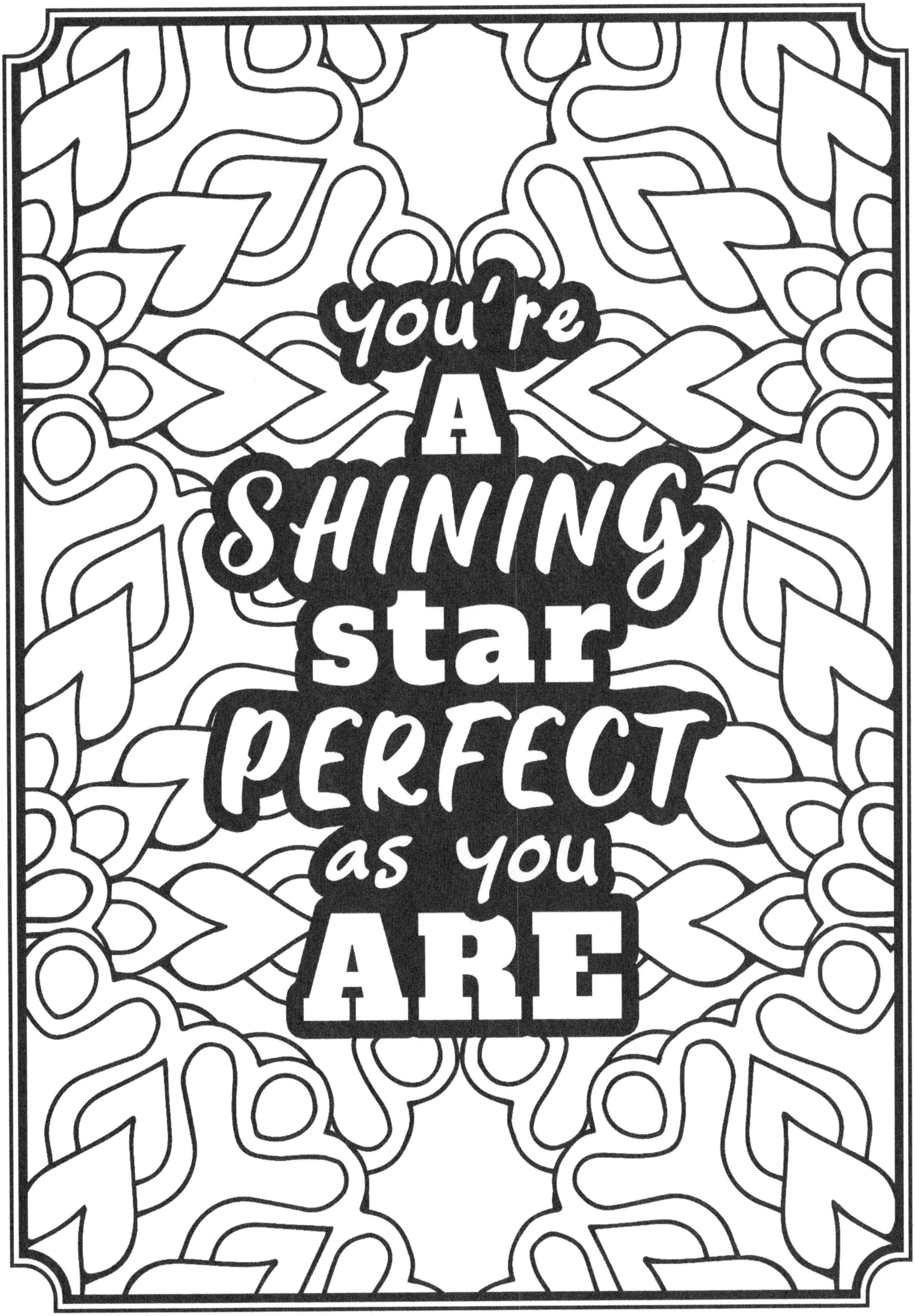
you're
A
SHINING
star
PERFECT
as you
ARE

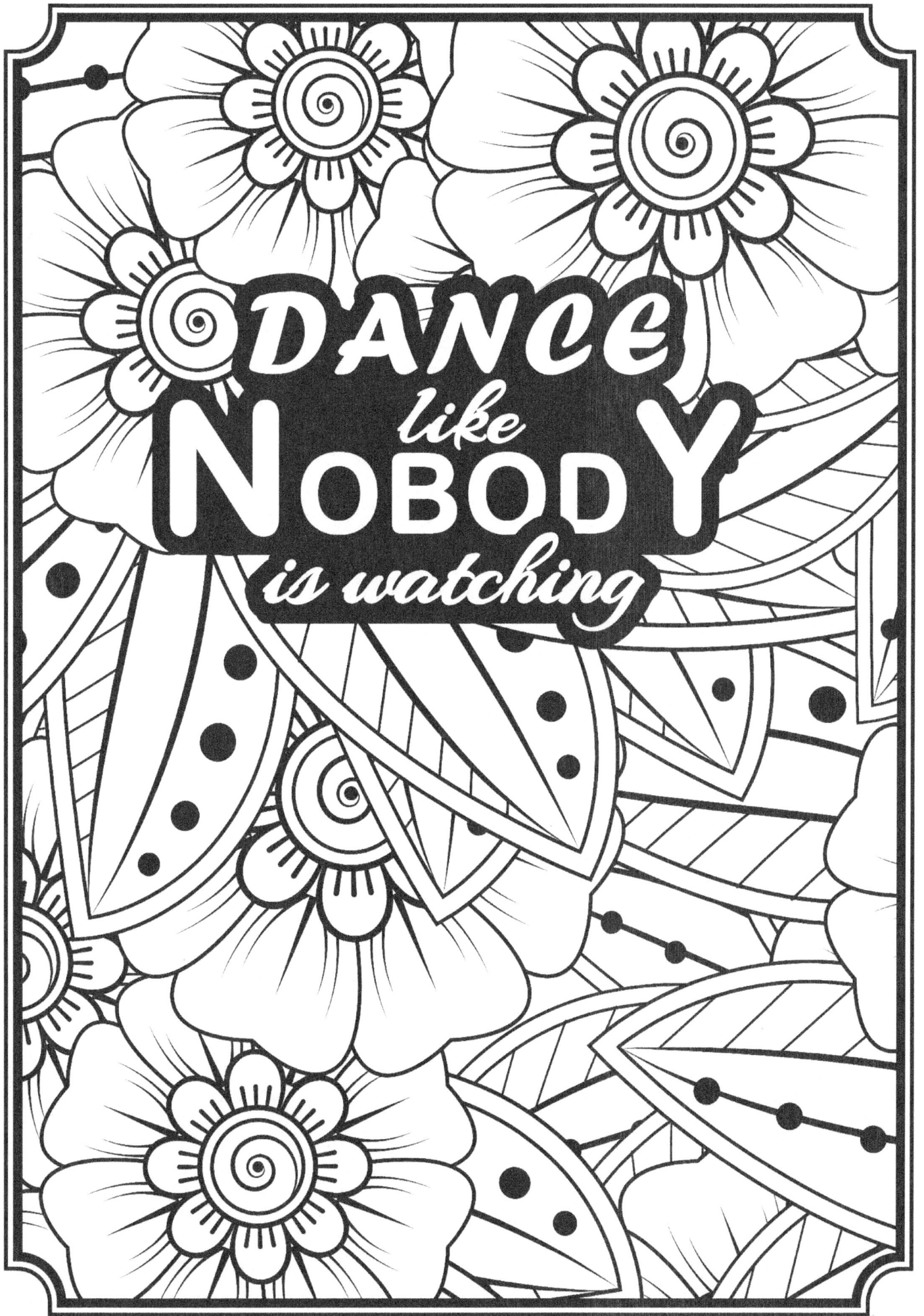

DANCE like NOBODY is watching

LOVE
& laughter
FILL **MY**
days

I BELIEVE in the Power of Kindness

sweet as
SUGAR
bright as a
RAINBOW

GLOWING
with
LOVE
and
JOY

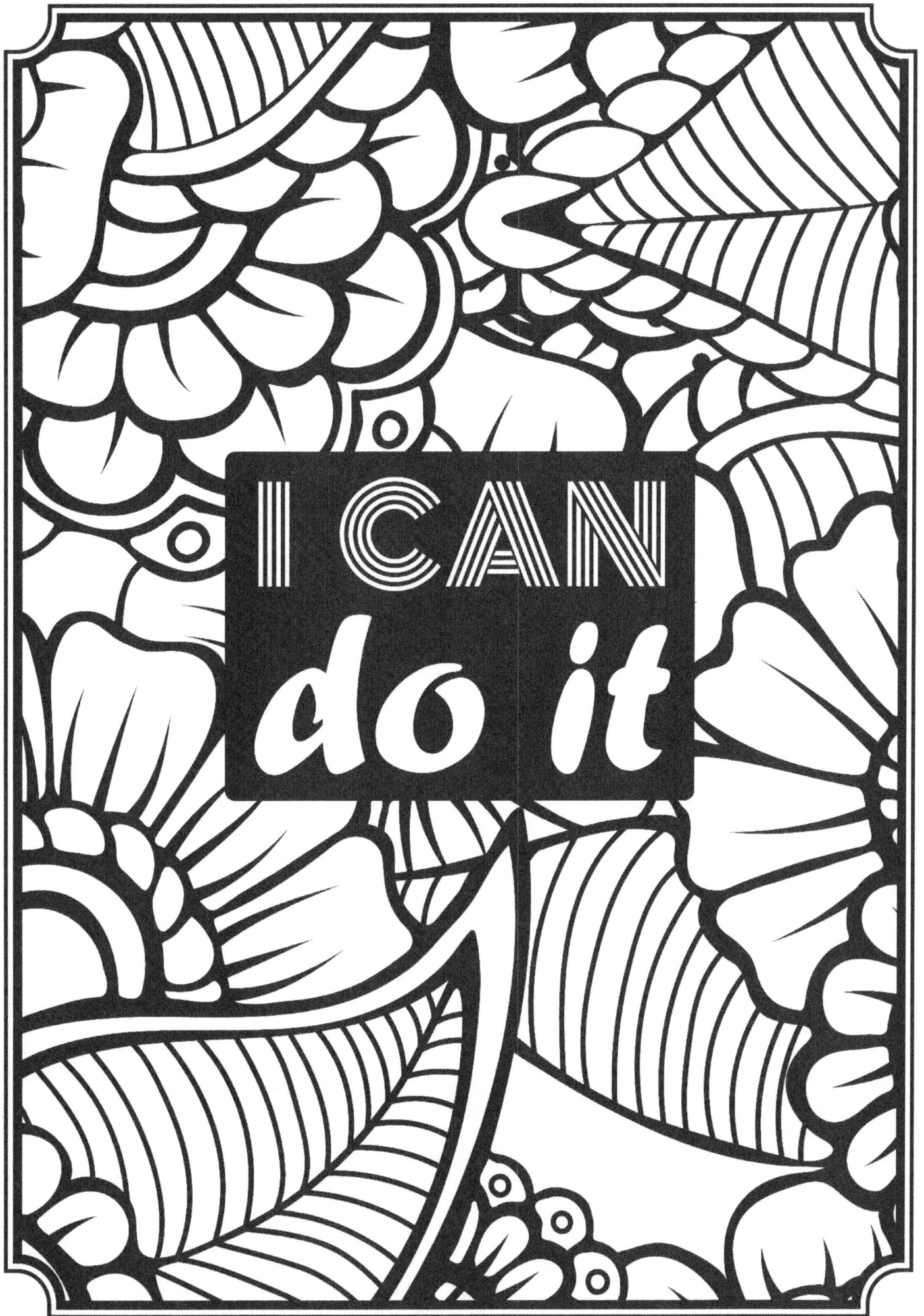

I CAN do it

I always TRY my BEST

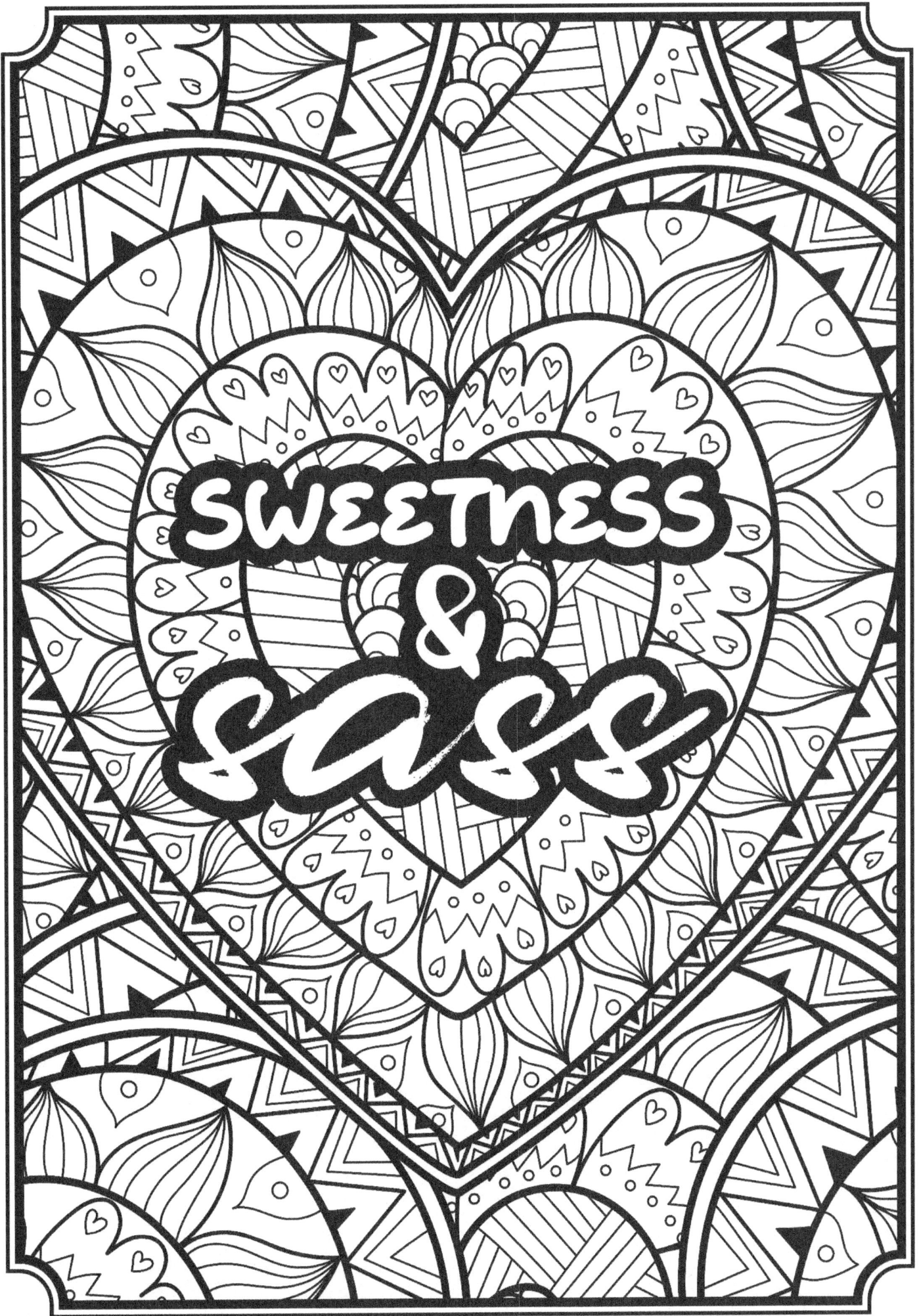
SWEETNESS & SASS

Printed in Dunstable, United Kingdom